Sight Word Tales ™

Some Dogs Are Very Good

by Mickey Daniels
illustrated by Richard Torrey

SCHOLASTIC INC.

New York • Toronto • London • Auckland • Sydney
Mexico City • New Delhi • Hong Kong • Buenos Aires

Designed by Maria Lilja
ISBN-13: 978-0-545-01659-9 • ISBN-10: 0-545-01659-2
Copyright © 2007 by Scholastic Inc.
All rights reserved. Printed in China.

First printing, November 2007

12 11 10 9 8 7 6 5 4 3 2 1   7 8 9 10 11 12/0

Sight Words

Sight words are words that you see again and again when you read. This book is filled with the sight words **some**, **very**, **good**, and **but**. Look for them in the text. Check the pictures, too!

Some dogs are **very good** at doing tricks.

But not Spot.

Some dogs are **very good**
at fetching sticks.

But not Spot.

Some dogs are **very good** at staying clean and neat.

But not Spot.

Some dogs are **very good** at waiting for a treat.

But not Spot.

Some dogs are **very good**—
as **good** as **good** can be.

But not Spot.

Spot is **very good** at being Spot.

But that is **good** enough for me!

Sight Word Review

Do you know the four sight words
in this book? Read aloud
the word on each flower.

good

some

some

but

very

very

good

but

Sight Word Fill-ins

some very
good but

Listen to the sentences. Then choose a sight word from the box to fill in each blank.

Word Box   **some**   **very**   **good**   **but**

1 This soap smells _____.

2 Try _Same_ of this pie.

3 That dog is _very_ cute.

4 She likes snakes, _but_ he does not.

5 May I borrow _some_ of your paper?

6 He is _good_ at spelling.

7 Everyone went outside _but_ me.

8 This box is _very_ big.

Sight Word Cheer

**Celebrate the new sight words
you learned by saying these
four short cheers.**

S-o-m-e! Give a yell!
What do these four letters spell?
A sight word that we all know well —
Some, some, some!

V-e-r-y! Give a yell!
What do these four letters spell?
A sight word that we all know well —
Very, very, very!

G-o-o-d! Give a yell!
What do these four letters spell?
A sight word that we all know well —
Good, good, good!

B-u-t! Give a yell!
What do these three letters spell?
A sight word that we all know well —
But, but, but!